DISC INTERIORS | PORTRAITS OF HOME

DISC INTERIORS

PORTRAITS OF HOME

DAVID DICK & KRISTA SCHROCK

RIZZOLI

TO PAUL, RJ, AND OUR FAMILIES

CONTENTS

INTRODUCTION

"Shelter" is a word we've been hearing with greater frequency, even urgency, over the last year, and it's one that has a slightly different meaning for each of us.

It's a noun, meaning a literal roof overhead or a metaphorical safe haven. It's a verb, referring to the act of taking refuge or protecting something from external forces. Every house is a shelter, technically speaking. But not every house makes its occupants feel sheltered, calm, secure, enveloped, safe. Conjuring those feelings out of a simple dwelling, composed of the same common materials as any other dwelling—cement, wood, plaster, tile, stone, fabric, and paint—requires a kind of alchemy that is difficult to describe. When you step across the threshold of a home that gets it right, you just know. It feels good, like a sigh of relief.

I've had that sensation many times over the last year as I wandered through the halls of homes designed by Krista Schrock and David John Dick of DISC Interiors. David and Krista, the founders and principal designers of DISC, understand the idea of shelter better than any designers I know.

We met nearly a decade ago when their business and friendship were both still forming. I was working as a design editor at a magazine here in Los Angeles. They had just finished collaborating on a remodeled 1920s bungalow in Los Feliz. They sent some photos and a description of it in a gently worded email, and my interest was piqued. Designer homes in L.A. often involve massive chandeliers, statuary around a pool, and a screening room for twenty, and this modest but perfect house was chic and cozy, the antidote to the Bel Air and Pacific Heights mansions I scrolled through in my Dropbox folders. I had met David and Krista around town, and my first impression was that they were kind and soft-spoken, increasingly rare qualities both in their chosen field and in the world at large. When I saw them at the shoot it was clear that their talents were many and varied. They had obvious expertise when it came to selecting soft, muted finishes, appealing textures, and tonal palettes that were neutral but never drab. Their taste was disciplined but not strict, unpretentious, and not easily time-stamped. I guess that I mistook their quiet confidence for experience, because I had no idea that this house was the first project they worked on together, as a team, until after the photos were taken. Luckily for all of us, it wasn't the last.

Here in Los Angeles, subtlety is rarely rewarded. The interior design world is no exception to that rule. Despite this truth, DISC has thrived. Over the years, Krista and David have transformed dozens of homes for creative couples and families to beautiful effect, many of which have been photographed for this book. Their work isn't merely decorative, meaning that they aren't afraid to tear down a wall or add a wing, if necessary. And there is no element, a hinge or a doorknob, that isn't carefully, painfully considered. Their clients are people who understand their true value as storytellers, creating a narrative about them as they furnish their rooms, and as advocates who interact with builders and makers on their behalf. While Krista and David's combined taste is what initially attracts clients to DISC, it's their unfailing kindness and calm demeanor that seals the deal.

Part of their magic is that they manage to imbue all of their projects with positivity, plastering it into the walls and stitching it into the seams of every cushion. When I visited the homes they designed while we were working on this book, I could often pick out the house on the block without even looking at the street numbers. Pardon the extreme California-ness of this next comment, but all of them had a kind of energy around them. You can tell that they were built with love.

That sense of security and comfort was apparent from the first step inside the front door, and we hope it emanates from the pages of this book in your hands.

—CHRISTINE LENNON

CHRISTINE LENNON: So we should start at the very beginning. Tell me again how you met. And how did you decide to work together?

DAVID JOHN DICK: We sort of met online [laughs]. But not really. It was 2011, although it feels like much longer. It's strange how quickly a decade of working together can pass. At that point, Krista was working for an interior designer and I was back at school at UCLA in their interiors program. I was also doing a bit of design writing for different interior style magazines such as *Remodelista* and *Apartamento*, and my own art/design blog. It was the early days of blogs, and I was totally absorbed into this portal of Tumblrs and design blogs and connecting to other designers by interviewing them. It was sort of an incubation time for me, slowly changing career paths. What I realized was that I really wanted to be a designer—not a writer. I just wasn't sure how I would get there. A friend had opened a new store on Beverly Boulevard, and he mentioned that a friend of his, Krista, was working on launching an interiors magazine. I went to the launch party she threw in downtown L.A., but I never got a chance to say hello. We managed to connect a few weeks later over lunch in Silver Lake, not far from where our office is now.

KRISTA SCHROCK: I had been working for a few design firms over the course of many years and I felt like I was finally ready to branch out on my own. I knew that I wanted a partner. This business requires a lot of diverse knowledge and wearing many hats. I know my strengths and weaknesses, and I wanted to work with someone who would complement what I do well and support me in areas that aren't as strong. I come from a family of entrepreneurs, so starting my own business felt like a natural progression for me. But I also felt that I needed to learn the business through hands-on experience in a design office, develop the skills on the job, and that would greatly improve the chances at success.

CL: *Collected*, your magazine, was a passion project, a kind of kitchen-table magazine that you and a friend pulled together, right?

KS: Yes. I had a partner, Jessica, who I worked with who also

IN THE CIRCLE

had a graphic design background, and we were both interior designers at the time. We had seen other digital interiors magazines and nothing really resonated with us. We wanted to showcase another side of design, something that was a bit cleaner in its aesthetic, focusing on the idea of refined living that was more minimal, but also warm and layered. We were drawn to the same influences and had many shared interests, such as Scandinavian design, Japanese wabi-sabi, great packaging, and neutral palettes. We also wanted to highlight some local L.A. designers, their homes and businesses. It was a similar idea to what photographer Todd Selby does with The Selby, offering a glimpse into the homes of L.A. "creatives." It felt like a good jumping off point to start a digital magazine, but we only made it for one issue. Once we realized how much work it was, I was like, "What are we doing?!" We were producing our own original photography, writing, graphic design, and it was just too daunting.

CL: What did you study in school, Krista? What was your passion?

KS: As a kid, I wanted to be a professional snowboarder, but I obviously did not do that [laughs]. Out of high school, I went to college to study geology, but eventually I realized that wasn't the right fit. What I really wanted was a creative career, and I really enjoyed design and languages and I left my home state of Pennsylvania to come to Los Angeles to study graphic design. I started working in a large corporation as a graphic designer after I graduated. I knew almost instantly that that kind of environment wasn't right for me. I discovered early on that I don't play office politics well. Also, graphic design felt very singular and a little isolating. It was a lot of time working in front of a computer alone and I found that I work better with a team.

CL: Were you craving a more collaborative environment?

KS: Yes, and I needed to do something more tactile and hands on, something that combined my love of design, sourcing, and creating something that was longer lasting, something that could get better as the years went by. One day, I was looking at *InStyle* magazine's home magazine, and I saw a designer's work in it that I loved. For the first time, I saw that interior

design could be a real career. So, I wrote to her and asked if she was looking for help, and that's how I got started. I worked for that firm, which introduced me to a new world of vintage furniture, art, and textiles I never knew existed. One of the highlights working in this firm was a trip to New York City to preview the Chandigarh sale at Christie's in 2007. That was my first introduction to Le Corbusier and Pierre Jeanneret, designers who I admire for their simplicity of form and materials. It was a pivotal experience for me to see the designs of these iconic designers in the sale preview and learn about the history of their experience working in India, their family connection, and how the furniture that was designed for Panjab University at Chandigarh, which many felt had no sense of aesthetic beauty, would become such collectible furniture. We sat in on the auction and bought a few pieces for clients. It was a thrilling experience and was the start of a deep appreciation for vintage furniture and design. Now when I look back, it feels like I was always seeking out interior design. Even growing up, I loved designing my bedroom and picking out wallpaper. I loved going to thrift stores and finding little treasures. It was a natural fit.

CL: We've talked about this before, but if you don't grow up in New York or L.A., or any of the major cities in the world, you might not think an interior design career is an option for you. If you're a kid in Kansas like me, or in Pennsylvania like you or Tennessee like David, you might not think you could ever be a part of that world. How about you, David? How did you get here?

DJD: I didn't even consider interior design for a career until I was in my mid-thirties. I had jumped into lots of different careers over the years, but none of them felt right to me long-term. I studied glassblowing, went back to school for psychology, and spent a few years in the wine world. My mom was always very creative when I was growing up. She not only loved to decorate and keep a house, but she excelled at it. She's not a decorator by trade, but I always tell her that she could have done it easily, if she had chosen to. I have vivid memories of *Southern Living* magazines piled high in baskets in our living room, ready to topple over. My parents would venture out to the estate sales on the weekend, searching for antiques and enjoying the hunt. She was always educating her eye, reading, experimenting with new pieces in our home, and traveling. So, I was always exposed to her creativity and ability to create a home, and it left its mark on me. But it's fair to say that it's not what I wanted to do—at all. I rebelled against it for many years, this idea of creating a home. I was much more interested in contemporary art, looking to painters and sculptors, and searching for other creative outlets. Then when I turned thirty, I really felt like a failed artist and sort of freaked out.

CL: I hate to hear you say failed, because all of the things that you've attempted and learned throughout your life led up to this moment. The art world is so commodified that if you don't make a million dollars selling your work you're seen as a failure. I don't buy it. If you made work that you loved, you're not a failure.

DJD. That's true, though with art I also realized that I didn't want to sit in a studio by myself all day. I love to be more collaborative, and art for me never utilized the different sides of my personality. I'm not sure why I couldn't make it work, it just didn't. To me, art feels more internal, something needing to be expressed. It comes from within, and that overwhelmed me, the challenge of figuring out what I would want to express. I think of design as solving a problem. It gives me parameters to work from, and there is something really appealing to me in that, collaborating with clients and telling their stories.

CL: I guess that's where the psychology part factors in.

DJD: It's less about me, and always about the clients first. I find that refreshing, though challenging at times. I'm not going to lie.

CL: Do you remember any design influences from your childhood that had an impact on you?

DJD: I was always observing the homes in our neighborhood, when we took walks around the block on summer evenings. The shapes of the rooflines, the colors of the brick exteriors, the simple paneling of a front door, an outdoor lantern, a glowing singular lamp in the front window. But I never truly thought much about it. Inside our home, I curiously watched my mom as she traversed through different phases of decorating.

For years, she'd pull in country and Amish influences into details, and I never really understood what that meant until we took a detour once on a family vacation to an Amish town, witnessing carpenters crafting pine benches in their work studios off the main square. In our kitchen at our home, we had an old wooden ice box that she had repurposed, and it was where she stored canned pickled vegetables from the garden, along with old photo albums. On the kitchen counter, there was a lamp with an intricately made paper shade. It had these vignettes that were illuminated by pinholes. She would change the lamp shades with the seasons. Not sure why, but I never really forgot those lampshades, and the changing of the lampshades.

CL: You understood the craftsmanship behind them, maybe.

DJD: Yes, I think so. It also helped me to understand and to feel how comfortable a home could be, and the stories a home can hold. It wasn't until many years later when I started to reflect on that, the comfort and subtle details that are present in a well-crafted home, and how much work is involved in pulling it all together. She made it look so effortless, like it had always existed, but it also expressed her point of view, her curiosity, her looking out into the world and then reflecting it inward, back into our home.

CL: Krista, I hear David say Amish and I think of Pennsylvania. Where in the state did you grow up?

KS: I'm from western Pennsylvania, so I grew up in Amish country. I have strong memories of going to the Amish country store down the country road, where craftsman would be making willow rockers, and their wives would have just baked pies and cookies that were for sale. My family's homes always centered around a big kitchen table where my relatives would gather for coffee and pie. Also, my grandparents, my mom, and my aunts were all very creative and into decorating their homes. Creating spaces that were warm, comfortable, and pleasing to the eye but also reflected that Amish country aesthetic.

CL: How does your relationship with nature influence your thinking about interior design?

KS: Nature really comforts me, and being in nature brings people together in a different way. I think people let their guard down when they are surrounded by nature, and it's a good way to get people to talk about what makes them happy at home. These elements can start the conversation about how a home feels and how it can reflect the client, which is what the essence of interior design is, to create a home for someone. I think the rich color palettes and textures of nature have been such a huge influence in the designers I admire but also the designs we create for clients. This signifies home to me, and comfort. Where I grew up, there are fields with old, rustic barns that are all falling apart and I love those. I could take photos of old barns all day! There's something so comforting about them, the patina of the wood and the faded paint. I love that feeling of worn patina, and that is a big influence in my approach to interior design.

CL: I'm a fellow barn fanatic so I get it. How would you describe your approach to working with clients?

KS: It is an intuitive thing. It's a feeling when you meet someone and how you will work with them, because everyone has a different approach to how they want the process to go. Some people can read plans, others can't. Some love the decorative part and would rather not think about the construction part, but what it does come down to is to really listen to what a client has to say. I think I'm a really good listener, and I think part of being an interior designer is to understand people, and who they really are, and oftentimes without knowing them for a very long period of time. You have to listen to what they're saying, and then distill what they actually mean. This is the hard part because it is a bit of a game in the beginning to figure out who they are. Once that part is established, we have a great process in presenting to clients that has been really effective to communicate the design intentions and help them to see that and feel confident moving forward.

CL: I'm fascinated with this part of your job, relating to clients. How do you gain someone's trust, in the beginning?

KS: Listening gains trust and vice versa. It can be stressful, having to be creative for someone else. We all have an idea of how living in a home should be, but you don't always want to talk about where the hampers should be. The best design is achieved when function and form are combined in such a way that it creates a wonderful home. When you are in a space that looks exceptional and functions well, to me, those are the best spaces. I think the common thread that connects most of our clients is that they are design minded. They care about their spaces and how they feel in their homes, but they have families and lives that require function. All of that needs to be discussed at the beginning of the process and not treated as an afterthought. Building and creating a home for a client is very similar to painting a portrait of them. At first, it doesn't really make sense, you see it but it's kind of a vague idea to the client and it is not fully formed. The more you work at it, develop it, and layer it, the better it gets. This is important to us as a firm.

DJD: Our clients' homes should reflect who they are, not who we are. We're open to shifting styles for our clients, always taking the time to know them, letting it unfold slowly. We're filtering design through our clients' eyes and lives. This is when the process gets richer and more varied.

KS: It's kind of a funny thing being an interior designer, when you're invited into these very intimate spaces. Even if we don't end up working with a client, we get to know people very quickly. Just stepping into a person's home you learn a lot about them.

DJD: It's true, there are few things I love more than seeing how people live in their personal spaces. It's endlessly fascinating, the private spaces we all exist in. I've always considered myself an introvert. The older I get, the more I realize how our homes and private spaces truly are the best portraits of our inner lives.

CL: Let's talk about some specifics of your work. I hear you talk about texture a lot. Why is it important? And what kind of texture are you drawn to?

DJD: Texture, to me, is the tactility of fabric or even stone, how it feels and massages your feet in the entryway, how the plaster on the walls absorbs the sunlight through the texture of the paint. We usually lean away from perfect finishes, finishes that are glossy and will leave a mark if touched. They can make you fearful that you're going to leave a ring or ruin something. We never want to create homes that you're afraid to touch and live in. Things that feel good to the touch appeal to us. The homes we design, we expect them to patina with time. If you come in with some built-in texture, it just brings depth and soul to a home. It sets up the home for success.

KS: Yes, absolutely. I couldn't agree more.

DJD: Texture is about playing around, mixing metals and finishes like aged brass and pewter, figuring out how to make things feel fresh yet lasting. We love to mix different fabrics together, seeing how they react and respond to each other. Textures are tools for creating something our client hasn't seen before. We really love this sense of experimentation in our studio, trying out combinations and seeing if they are successful.

CL: I like how you frame that. Playing with textures and coming up with unexpected combinations is what makes a room feel so unique. You may have seen that chair before, but you may not have seen it with a leather cushion. This is the stuff that requires a sure hand, and what you do so well.

KS: I also think of textures as being a tactile thing but texture can also mean stimulating different senses. There might be a candle burning in a room and the scent adds a layer and you have levels of lighting that create a warm glow in a room. So you have these textures with fabric and rugs, but you also incorporate the other senses. A space with texture envelopes you. That's something we're striving for, too.

CL: How you treat stone, whether you polish or hone it, and the metal finishes you choose, that all adds to texture as well, correct?

DJD: Ilse Crawford talks a lot about touch in one of her books, and I've never stopped thinking about it. This idea of consciously simply touching everything in your home. What does it make you feel? How do you feel when you sit on your sofa? Does a chair encourage you to read a book in it? The warmth and feel of a piece of hardware in your kitchen, when you pull open the drawer. It's a sense of awareness, being awake to your senses. To me, that's what textures are. Putting thought into every finish in a home, whether it's a simple hand towel or a handwoven throw over a linen sofa, it will make a space feel different when you touch it. For us, we aim to orchestrate all of those textures into a story line that's appropriate for the client, the architecture, for the location of the house and the neighborhood. It's a bit like a puzzle, to find the right pieces that fit.

CL: It's a lot to think about when you're working from top to bottom in a house, to make it feel cohesive. The right finish or color can invite you down a hallway, or make you want to examine something more closely. I'm always walking through a house and pawing everything to see how it feels! If I come to your house and grope your upholstery, consider it a compliment.

KS: Me too. I love so many fabrics. I'm very much into textiles, that's my thing! I am influenced by the great textile designers like Kay Sekimachi for her use of muted color in her weaving, but also the incorporation of natural elements like leaves in what she creates. I really connect to textiles because I like that the wool or cotton was harvested by hand. There is a primitive element to textiles, as well, because there is this idea of using your hands to create something someone will love for years. I love antique textiles, Japanese textiles and Indian textiles the most. Growing up, we had quilts on all of our beds. My grandmother was very into quilting. The process of making a quilt in a community, sitting quietly or with family and creating these quilts for special occasions, or for your own home, is so special and appealing. The patterns all had specific meaning, and they were constructed out of scraps of fabric that would create fascinating color combinations.

CL: Fabric is often the finishing touch of a project though, right?

KS: Yes, texture for me starts with textiles, but when you're building a home, the fabric selection doesn't happen until far down the road. From the beginning of the process, I'm always thinking about fabrics but also thinking about metal, stone, and brick, and then how to layer the texture of fabric on top of that. I love linens, wools, and bouclés. I love leathers—something a little softer balanced by something a little cooler. I gravitate toward vendors who create beautifully woven fabrics such as Rogers & Goffigon, Mark Alexander, or Designs of the Time. Rose Uniacke's new line of textiles are so sumptuous to the touch and the colors are just so good. I also shy away from busy patterns and tend to gravitate toward patterns that are neutral or more calm, that create a feeling of stillness, that enhance a texture, maybe that even look more like a texture than a pattern. I want a room to reveal itself over time. As you look more, you see things that were not apparent before, that make you want to dive in and touch things, and investigate the space a bit more. Textiles create this curiosity for me.

CL: It takes a certain confidence to back away from pattern, to walk away from a lot of print and let a room be the purest expression of itself. There's a visual busy-ness that you guys are very good at avoiding. How do you know when to stop?

KS: Editing is really something we've gotten good at. We will introduce a lot of ideas for patterns, textures, colors in the beginning but we always edit backward. It's also very important to think about the space holistically and how each space flows from one room to another. We'll ask ourselves, "What are we layering these textiles on? Is the rug neutral? Does it have a pattern? Is it colorful? What is the chair and sofa upholstered in?" Maybe a vintage leather chair doesn't need a pillow. We really want everything to harmonize and feel balanced. I think this harmony creates a calmness that can be hard to achieve without editing. Nothing should scream "look at me." That's one thing that we constantly hear our clients comment to us, that our spaces feel very edited. Especially when you are working around a bold art collection, which our clients often have. You can't have too much pattern in those rooms.

CL: Do you find that you have similar instincts when it comes to editing? Do you ever disagree when one of you says, "We're done now?" Or do you both know when to say when?

KS: In general, I do think that we both know when to stop. We really strive to find pieces that feel unique and maybe haven't been seen a thousand times. We like shopping at the same vendors time and time again, and David and I have gotten very good at homing in on the same piece of furniture while we shop for clients. It's really an instinctual thing that develops when you work with someone for so many years. I really am amazed by it sometimes.

DJD: It's true. I used to find it odd that we have a certain sense of designer ESP that happens, but now I find it comforting. And we respect each other. We've created a circle that, I think, allows us both to feel very creative. We rarely disagree inside the circle.

CL: How do you divide the tasks? Do you say, "I'll take the master, and you take the dining room," and then talk about ideas?

KS: Usually, we divide it up in terms of construction and decoration. David usually handles the construction-related projects. He'll have the bones of a kitchen design, working through construction details, but then we'll look at it together and discuss what is working and what is not. There's a collaborative process in all of the design. And we talk a lot and look at images, discuss them and break them apart. It energizes us to work together. We respect each other's creative vision. We have different points of view and backgrounds that inform the process, and a balance of masculine and feminine energy. I think clients find both of our energies comforting.

DJD: With a small office, we are all wearing different hats every day. We are dedicated to remaining a small office, so we each are able to have our own voice present in the projects. Every one of our designers in the office also brings their own expertise and experience to the project, which also brings richness and technical knowledge. I think one of the best parts of the job is coming to work with a family you worked to create, a place that nourishes, as opposed to a place that breaks people down. We love being introduced to new ideas, new ways of living. It's important for our office to be a place that is encouraging of expressing ideas. Design is competitive, stressful, and you can feel deflated sometimes, but we always love to laugh.

CL: Another word I hear a lot around interior design "narrative," or storytelling. How do you tell a story through interior design?

DJD: Narrative begins from listening to clients. We have to ask ourselves, "What is their story?" You feel it when you walk in some homes, this pure expression of who someone is. We encourage people to look a bit inward, pull things from their past, and incorporate it into the design, so the home feels part of their own unique history. I always think about who the client is and where they are from. Do they long for that place? Do they want something that's a real departure from what they grew up with, or something familiar? Who do they want to be? We will often work with couples who have styles that are not exactly the same, so there can be a bit of a tug of war between the two. The challenge is assuring them that the house can represent both of their narratives. It does not have to be a compromise. That is what will make the house feel unique.

CL: Are there iconic designers and architects that you're constantly going back to for inspiration?

DJD: I've always been drawn toward artists and designers who have a philosophical or emotional bent to their work. Louise Bourgeois's works have always been incredibly meaningful to me. I love her ability to meld her personal history into her art, and her ability to express emotions through different mediums like marble, embroidered fabrics, sketches, wire, and text. Felix Gonzalez-Torres's work was an early inspiration for me. He spoke about personal loss through conceptual minimalism, using everyday objects such as candy and lightbulbs. Also, both Lucian Freud and Francis Bacon, the painters, for the intensity of their portraits and the depth of their colors. And Charles Rennie Mackintosh, the architect, Axel Vervoordt, and Picasso.

KS: It changes for me as I am still learning, but I love Agnes Martin's minimal and clean aesthetic, but I can flip it and go crazy for William Morris prints and patterns. I secretly want to own an English country house which is just layered from floor to ceiling in pattens on pattern. We both really love Ilse Crawford, and she is always talking about how spaces make you feel. When I went to Stockholm, I stayed at a hotel she designed called Ett Hem. It was one of the best hotel experiences I have had. The hotel is in a home in a residential neighborhood of Stockholm. The large brick building with a copper verdigris roof is quite striking, and a red brick fence surrounds the property. From the moment you walk into the courtyard, you are transported to this fantasy life. The reception area and shared lounge space is painted this warm shade of gray, and there are velvet sofas, fuzzy chairs, worn-in leather, just layers upon layers of comfort. It is all so beautiful, no detail is spared. Everything texture I love in a space is in that hotel, with a shared kitchen and library with so many books to peruse. There's sensuality and feeling, and the fields of space are

so enveloped. Crawford's work, especially this property, has been such a strong influence for me. She reinforces the importance of layering materials and creating unique details that make a space memorable. I also really connect to Roman and Williams for their love of nature and history. There's always a natural element to their spaces, which I just adore. A structure's history and sense of place is always so strong and considered when they design, and I really connect to that.

CL: I'm sure that whenever you travel, you're always thinking about how to bring some of those elements you experience back home. How do you think travel informs your style?

KS: To me, the travel influences come out in the details. Maybe there's a tile pattern, or a brick pattern in a sidewalk, that we can incorporate into a new construction to make it feel less brand-new. If you can usher in a sense of history it helps to make a house feel less sterile. And I have always been drawn to Denmark and the great Danish designers like Hans Wegner and Frits Henningsen. I never tire of it. That always feels fresh to me. Japan was also a travel highlight for me. There are so many concepts and ideas in Japanese life that appeal to me, one being wabi-sabi, the idea of imperfect beauty. I really love having something in a room that just feels a little old and crusty, something that feels like it could fall apart at any minute. It reminds me that life is fragile and we must embrace and hold tight the things that are important to us.

DJD: I love traveling anywhere. Fez in Morocco really was a pivotal trip, and that trip made me realize how important it is to travel to places that call to you, even if you don't know why at the time. Trust your instinct. I love to simply walk in a new city, understanding how neighborhoods transition, how people are actually living. I love photographing and documenting what my eye is excited about, an architectural detail, the faded colors of a painted sign, or simply how tea is presented on an engraved brass tray.

CL: Bringing it back to L.A. design, this city has put itself on the map in the art world and the design world in recent years. This last decade has seen a lot of change. I'm wondering how you've seen it evolve.

DJD: The art world has diffused into the design world, and there is a real design renaissance happening here. There is this sense of the new, and definite youthful energy in L.A. at the moment—but we'll have to see how it ages. As excited as I am about the contemporary design world, I feel like I am at the age when I am spending more time looking backward, a bit more nostalgic. Lately I find myself more intrigued by the historical homes and researching the architectural history of Los Angeles than I do at the latest design fair.

KS: It's exciting to live in a city that has an emerging creative culture in design and art. There are so many great makers here, and it's been fun to become friends with so many of them. In terms of furniture design that's coming out now, it's been more of a struggle for me to connect to some of this new wave of design. I always wonder, "Who will want to sit in this chair?" It doesn't always make a lot of sense to me. For me, comfort is really a priority and it feels like some of the newer design is for show. It feels disposable in a way. I like things that stand the test of time.

CL: When you're shopping for furniture, what qualities do you look for in a piece?

DJD: It really depends on the client and the room. There are so many variables. Not all pieces in a room need to be the "star," and by that I mean selecting pieces for a home is sometimes like selecting the cast of a film. There are leading roles and supporting roles. I am always telling clients that not every piece in a room needs to be a star! Rooms that feel over-designed and trying too hard feel inauthentic to me. I am always looking at the shape of a piece of furniture and visualizing how it will work with all of the other pieces in a room. How do we create harmony with different combinations of furniture? We are constantly touching everything, sitting in chairs, sitting on sofas in showrooms, really making mental notes about the specific piece of furniture. Comfort is key, but aesthetics of course matter. Dining chairs are a great example of this. To find the perfect dining chair, one that is comfortable and stunning, is not as easy as it sounds. A chair that you want to have a three-hour dinner in, and not have your lower back be numb, is a challenge to find.

CL: I think you're striving to be more timeless in your work overall, not easily date-stamped.

DJD: Design can't be just about what looks good in a photograph. L.A. is a city built on storytelling, and there's always an opportunity to live any life you want to. It's truly like no other city. But we want to build homes that last, create spaces for meaningful relationships to develop, rooms for conversations with family, places to linger, kitchens that really are meant to be cooked in, family rooms that have game tables and cozy chairs and soft lighting at night to read in. How do we further design homes that somehow are able to de-stress us and restore us? Maybe we will find some of these answers by looking backward rather than forward.

KS: To create a design that's new and fresh and different but also feels very old and has a sense of graceful age is the primary goal of our design firm. It's very important for us to tell a story that includes a timeless narrative. Trendy is not a word we use often. We value that ability to work with great artisans and collaborators and work with everyone on our staff who share a common vision. We want our clients to enjoy their experience working with us and sometimes you just have to remember that creating a home is supposed to be a joyful and pleasurable process!

1 | WINDSOR SQUARE

Of all of the visionaries who shaped domestic architecture in and around Los Angeles, few have a legacy as elegant and enduring as Paul R. Williams, the trailblazing Black architect who designed homes for Frank Sinatra and Lucille Ball, among many others. In Windsor Square, a tract of land in Hancock Park that is home to the Getty House (the official mayor's residence) as well as Norman and Dorothy Chandler's famous mansion "Los Tiempos," Williams's fingerprints are evident on nearly every street.

This stately French Chateau–style house is typical of his work, and is evidence of how easily a home with this kind of provenance can adapt to contemporary life. With such solid bones and timeless details, from the original fireplace mantel to the detailed dentil crown molding, the large-scale rooms could pass for a grand apartment in Paris. But the objects within, like the well-used record player in the living room, which regularly spins the owners' collection of indie rock vinyl, are accessories for a more relaxed life.

Adapting the same strategy used in architecturally classic homes with a modern sensibility in Europe, the rooms are furnished somewhat sparsely, letting cherished family heirlooms and a contemporary art collection with a strong point of view take center stage.

Custom upholstered pieces in a palette of handsome grays provide ample seating for entertaining and relaxing that doesn't compete with the art on the walls. Steel and glass doors in the rear of the room open to a patio and a swimming pool, with a great flow for hosting summer gatherings with friends and family.

To bring it all together in a cohesive mix, we turned to a few well-chosen anchors, like a bronze and brass cocktail table made in Umbria by Reschio, Gabriel Scott stools, and re-editions of Jean Royère chairs. In the more formal of the two dining rooms, watercolor-inspired wallpaper from Black Crow Studios and soft blush velvet draperies soften the sharper lines of the leather dining chairs and a Gio Ponti–designed table. A Swedish-inspired rug underfoot and a color palette of soft blues and blush add a feminine sensibility to this gorgeous, comfortable home.

2 | HANCOCK PARK

The thick plaster walls, generous windows, and sturdy tile rooftops in the homes that are popular throughout the Mediterranean are designed to keep interior rooms cool, which is why the architectural style—and Spanish-style homes in particular—make a lot of sense in the Southern California climate. The climates of Spain and Southern California are so similar that even trees native to Spain (almond, elm, citrus) thrive here. The style was especially popular in the 1930s, when some of the city's most elegant neighborhoods were developed. And this beautifully maintained Hancock Park mini-estate is a perfect example of it done well.

There were two contributing factors that made working on this home feel like a dream. First, the client owns a business that specializes in vintage and high-end flooring, reclaimed planks and tile, and had already created an impressive canvas of herringbone wood, rustic terra-cotta, and hand-finished surfaces for us to work with. Secondly, the exterior spaces were designed by Scott Shrader, who is one of the most notable landscape designers in Los Angeles. Shrader transformed the grounds into a hidden oasis in Hancock Park, the first suburb of downtown Los Angeles just a few miles to the east.

Our mission was to incorporate rustic, rough-hewn surfaces to create a relaxed elegance, inspired by modern European country houses. A color palette limited to the earthiest neutrals—bone, sand, clay, leather, blonde and dark wood, and khaki—let the built-in texture of the home, like the imported vintage mantelpiece and raw wood kitchen cabinetry, doors, and frames, take center stage.

Vintage French woven rattan kitchen chairs, a reclaimed oak dining table, a unique Swedish hutch in the dining room, and a hand-carved bench from Dos Gallos strike the right informal tone without compromising any elegance. In the master bedroom, an Indian bedcover, pale blush sheets, and a rich, mauve linen headboard have a sun-faded quality. The only saturated color in the house is found in the media room, with its tone-on-tone army green walls and drapery, which can be pulled shut to create a denlike hideaway.

3 | BRENTWOOD CANYON

Until the late 1970s and early 1980s, the exclusive Brentwood neighborhood, west of the famed 405 freeway, felt like a sleepy, bucolic suburb of Los Angeles, with a steady breeze off of the ocean and hawks soaring overhead. Jimmy Stewart was married in the Presbyterian church in the center of "town," but overall the area's Hollywood glamour is a more recent invention.

The appeal of the winding canyon roads that trace the hills of far west Los Angeles is undeniable. Each narrow lane is lined with beautiful houses of virtually every imaginable architectural style—Spanish colonial, stately Georgian, and classic Tudor houses from the '20s and '30s, as well as sleek steel and glass cubes. One style that appears to be pulling ahead of the pack with newly constructed homes is the modern traditional farmhouse. The typical features are towering windows to let in light filtered through the abundant surrounding greenery, seamed metal roofing, pale oak floors, and soaring ceilings.

With this house, we felt a real push/pull between the modern and traditional aspects of the design. Inside, elegantly worn vintage rugs placed around the home's large-scale rooms counter the brand-new feeling that is inherent in more recently built homes, creating a feeling of history and permanence. The earthy fawn shade in the dining room was another visual strategy intended to create a moodier cocoon of color that makes the room feel like a special destination slightly removed from the open foyer. The custom-designed Mira Mara multipendant fixture is the focal point of an elegant dining room. It is suspended over a round, blackened oak dining table that is surrounded by Thomas Hayes chairs. The tailored spareness of the architectural details, like paneled walls, crisp molding, and pristine, honed marble fireplace mantels, is balanced by welcome warmth that comes from the color palette of muted neutrals mixed with mauve, plum, and warm blues.

On the main level, we designed a game room for puzzles and card games over cocktails. A vintage chandelier we spotted on a trip to Copenhagen adds a grown-up sophistication to a typical family playroom. In the kitchen, a generous breakfast nook with extra-deep cushions was inspired by an oversized banquette spotted at a Parisian restaurant.

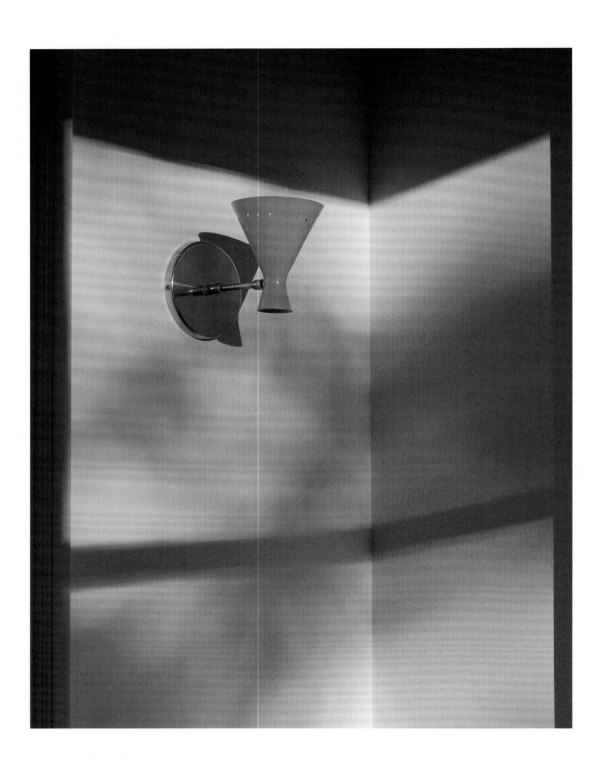

4 | SYCAMORE CANYON

Visitors to Los Angeles rarely get to see the very best of the city, which often lies at the end of a long driveway, behind a gate, or tucked away on a blink-and-you'll-miss-it side street. Savvy newcomers and lifelong Angelenos know that when someone invites you into their home, you say yes please and thank you, because that's where the best stories are told, and where the real beauty of this town can be found. This jewel-box, Wallace Neff house in a leafy grove near the beach is a perfect example of a hidden treasure, which we helped to reimagine in an extensive remodel.

It might not come as a surprise to learn that one of the owners of this four-bedroom house is English. Yes, the design is California to its core, from rich antique textiles from local legend Pat McGann to the romantic tiles that decorate the stairs, which were handmade by Forrest Lesch-Middelton, an artisan in Petaluma. But the kitchen, with its tall hood over the range, hand-finished limestone counter, colorful cabinets, and unique marble backsplash and countertops, feels like a tribute to a Cotswolds cottage.

The owners took a refreshingly practical approach to furniture and design. When we were choosing the breakfast table light fixture, they specified that it couldn't hang too low. "What if we want to move the table out of the way so the kids can dance?" they asked. Still, every room holds a treasure, like the Rose Tarlow lamps by the bedside in the master bedroom and vintage 1940s elevator sconces in the powder room. An empty crawl space on the second floor was transformed into a secret nook, which is wallpapered with a sweet floral pattern and filled with pillows, and accessed through a hidden door behind a bookcase. It's the preferred reading and dreaming spot for the family's two young daughters.

When furnishing a home, we love to select pieces that make a room feel like it has always been there, and create a blend of contemporary creature comforts like comfy sofas and accents like sculptural side tables. One of our favorite pieces in the home is a hutch in the dining room that is finished in gold leaf. We discovered it while staying at the Casamidy house in San Miguel de Allende, Mexico, and we hope will become a family heirloom.

Spanish Colonial Style
SANTA BARBARA AND THE ARCHITECTURE OF JAMES OSBORNE CRAIG AND MARY McLAUGHLIN CRAIG   SKEWES-COX / SWRINES   R

SHELTON, MINDEL & ASSOCIATES   ARCHITECTURE AND DESIGN   R

FROM THE LAND   The Architecture of Backen, Gillam & Kroeger   R

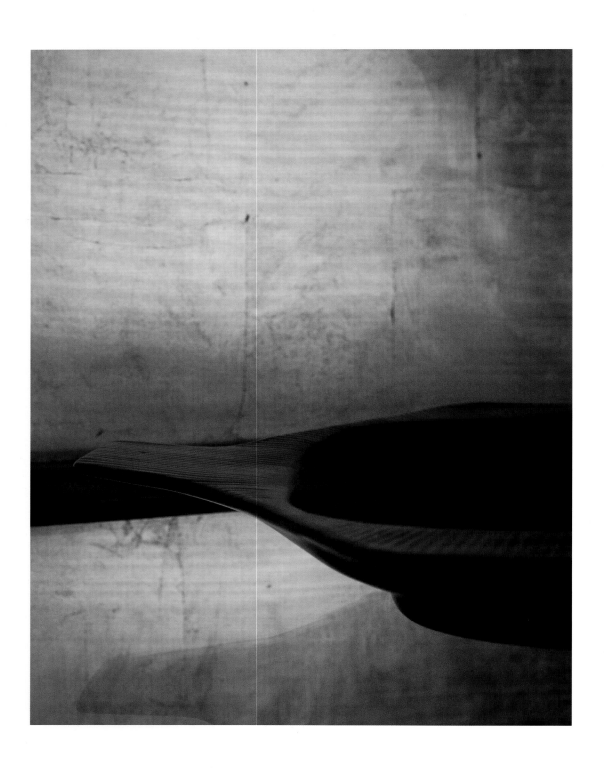

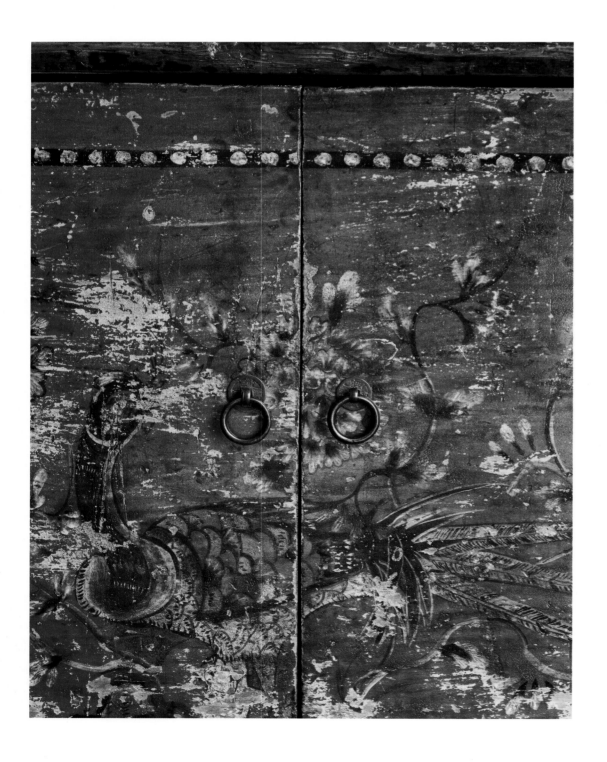

5 | BROOKSIDE

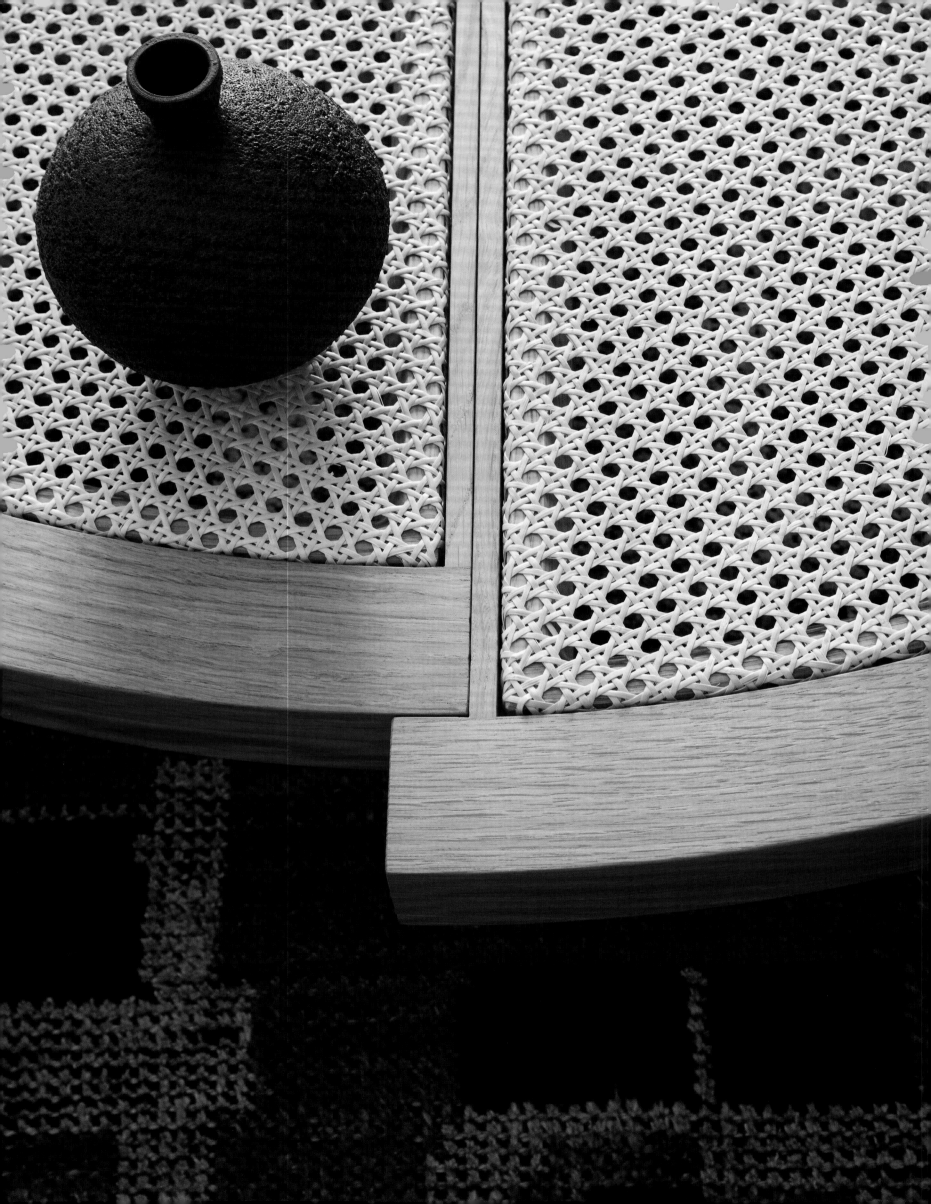

With its slender rooms and pocket-sized lot in Brookside, an under-the-radar neighborhood in central Los Angeles known for romantic backyard bridges that cross a small creek, this Spanish Colonial–style home packs in everything you could want from a grander house into a smaller footprint. The clients, a creative, well-traveled young family, often entertain music industry colleagues at home, so they needed a versatile space that would be both child-friendly and sophisticated. The previous owners had updated the kitchen and many of the surfaces with shinier, Hollywood Regency flair. Our goal was to dial back the bolder accents and create a more layered, bohemian atmosphere, minus any extraneous clutter.

Our work began in the entry, where we swapped out a black and white polished marble floor with a warmer mix of natural and black terra-cotta tile. To the right of the front entrance, a formal living room and more casual den are divided by a fireplace. The front room, with its graceful, pale coral curved sofa, traditional fireplace, and circular Charlotte Perriand cocktail table, opens up to an outdoor patio with a grand fountain, making it the perfect spot to gather year-round. In the more casual den in the rear, another custom sofa with French mattress tufting sits facing a French door that opens to the backyard and the pool. The ample light from windows on two sides make it the perfect nook for reading or quiet conversation. When the owners move the wicker Hollywood at Home coffee table to one side, it also functions as a makeshift yoga studio.

An intimate dining room with space for a table for six appears grander thanks to the Salvador Dalí sculpture in the corner and a flush mount Italian light fixture that takes up horizontal space, not vertical, so none of the ceiling height in the snug room is lost.

The combination of plum-colored bedding, a rust velvet accent pillow, and quiet, elegant blue walls and tonal window coverings make the master bedroom feel feminine but not frilly. Rugs from the owners' trip to Morocco anchor the sitting room and the master bedroom, adding another layer of personal expression to this collected home.

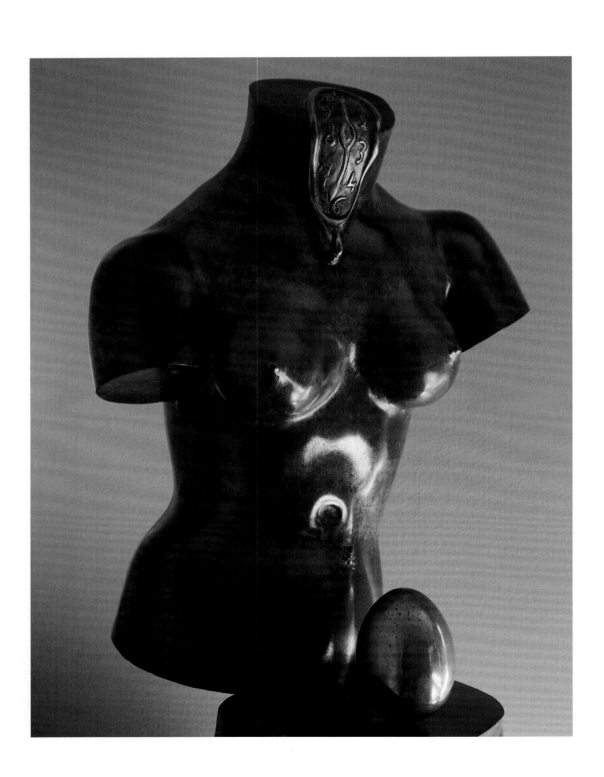

148

6 | HOLLYWOOD

ED RUSCHA

DAVID HOCKNEY A BIGGER EXHIBITION

George Condo

A N N I E L E I B O V I T Z

The tree-lined streets in and around Hollywood and its adjacent neighborhoods are paved with stories. Between 1910 and 1924, the population of Los Angeles tripled in size, growing from just over 300,00 residents to one million. Major film studios opened across town, and a residential building boom created tidy neighborhoods to house the influx of creative professionals. In recent years, homes like this single-story Tudor on the southern edge of Hollywood have seen a new wave of owners moving in and updating the layout for the needs of modern families, expanding the footprint to include larger closets, luxurious bathrooms, and more open floor plans that let the outside in.

Hancock Park–based June Street Architecture extended and redesigned this home, seamlessly adding a master suite with double-height ceilings and a wall of glass that opens onto a chic, narrow black-bottomed pool. The space above the garage was transformed into the perfect guest room, with a built-in reading nook and a cozy tree house feel under the eaves.

The interiors also reflect this blend of old and new, incorporating the owners' impressive contemporary art collection, intriguing textiles and tapestries, and handmade accents, like the three-foot-tall, hand-thrown Victoria Morris pottery lamp that glows warmly in the front window. The color palette, a mix of bone white, charcoal, and warm earth tones, punctuated by vintage leather and woven accents, is as subtle as can be. Classic mid-century shapes, like a Børge Mogensen leather sofa, share space with new work like ceramics from Michelle Quan and a sculptural light fixture by Michael Anastassiades.

BRAND-NEW & TERRIFIC ALEX KATZ IN THE 1950s

JOHN BALDESSARI PURE BEAUTY

SIGMAR POLKE MoMA

Aaron Garber-Maikovska   Being One And Then Sum

7 | SILVER LAKE HILLS

The creative legacy of Silver Lake, an artsy enclave on the eastern edge of Los Angeles, is long and varied, extending back to the silent movie era of the 1910s. Cecil B. DeMille, Charlie Chaplin, and Walt Disney all left their mark by building studios in the area, and it was one of the first LGBT-friendly communities in the United States back in the 1930s. Richard Neutra designed a row of modern masterpieces here in the fifties and sixties. To this day, creatives flock to the funky but increasingly refined homes that dot the hills.

When you see how serene and airy this Spanish colonial revival is now, it's hard to picture it as we saw it originally. It was a challenge to look past the cluster of small, dark rooms to see its potential as an all-white sanctuary, inspired by clean Belgian minimalism, with great 1920s bones.

We started by removing a few walls to open up the kitchen and living room and create a flow between living spaces. Another priority was to take advantage of its location high in the hills overlooking the Silver Lake Reservoir and let in the ample natural light that was available.

Stripping down the home to its barest essentials, like leaving the fireplace in its simplest form and building a tidy and functional kitchen, gave it a strong European feel. That was enhanced by pared-down pendants from Belgian ceramicist Jos Devriendt, which are suspended over the streamlined kitchen island, and the color palette and range of materials used, including natural linen upholstery, pale gray limestone countertops, bone-white plastered walls, oak planks, and basalt kitchen floors.

Accents like handmade South African baskets near the fireplace and woven leather dining chairs added some rusticity to the polished decor. Plush silvery rugs and twilight colors like pale pink and gray lend some welcome softness. And the nearly empty walls and ceilings become a kind of blank canvas for a light show, both natural and man-made. They change color as the sun moves across the sky, and the Pegasso vintage flush mount light in the master bedroom creates a star pattern on the ceiling when illuminated.

8 | HOLMBY HILLS

In a real estate market as competitive as the one in Los Angeles, home buyers often find themselves adjusting their "vision" of the perfect house in ways they never expected. The owners of this classic Georgian house in the exclusive, old-school Holmby Hills neighborhood had been hunting for something more in line with the rustic-modern French villa of their dreams. They had a binder full of collected photos, depicting a milk-toned sanctuary with oversized rooms and a classic, functional kitchen, which was far from the existing warren of smaller rooms with statelier accents they found in this house. What they saw in the house, primarily, was potential and a great address. People often wonder if they have permission to reimagine a house so dramatically, and fear that the interior will seem so alien from the home's facade that they appear at odds. In some cases, it doesn't make any sense. But for this house, which had not been updated in forty years, it was a welcome refresh.

We started by designing a new floor plan, which added a unique and stunning focal point—a glass-walled wine room to house a five-hundred-bottle collection—just off of the dining area. We kept the more formal details, like the classic paneled walls and the grand staircase, but stripped back one of the fireplaces and created more spacious but minimal bathrooms. A contemporary, open chef's kitchen has a new, massive marble-topped island lined with antique brass bar stools, upholstered in a durable Chris Barrett outdoor fabric. The softness of the upholstery, the warmth of the mixed metal fixtures (in polished nickel, steel, and aged brass), and the character of the English ceramic pendant lights from Hector Finch keep it all from appearing stark. A cloud gray front door, silvery green walls in the media room, and accents of deep blue punctuate the warm-white simplicity of the interiors with serene color.

Lastly, one of the perks of buying a house that you weren't expecting to love is that it might come with a feature you never knew you always wanted, like the snug built-in bar. We painted it a muted blush pink, chose pared-down bar stools, and installed a newly produced French rattan light fixture over a game table with classic Thonet caned chairs. Much to our clients' surprise, it has become one of their favorite spots to entertain.

9 | RUSTIC CANYON

This is the second property we worked on in Rustic Canyon, a leafy enclave in the Pacific Palisades, a place that encapsulates the very best of Los Angeles living: ocean breezes, easy access to hiking trails, and a feeling of privacy but not isolation. Just a block from the beach but hidden in the trees, this concrete, glass and steel house has an unexpected warmth that made it a soothing, fuss-free home base for a creative couple. Because they work in food and photography, two priorities for the homeowners were a beautiful, open, high-functioning kitchen and plenty of natural light.

The polished concrete floors and a 30-foot sliding glass door in the main living area give you the impression that you're in an urban artist's loft placed in the middle of a verdant canyon. Textured walls and ceilings finished with New Mexican clay, a wall of linen drapery, a plush wool rug, and an extra-long and deep sofa add a soft contrast to the steel and stone. The kitchen, with its matte oak cabinetry, burnished brass hardware, and a long stone countertop with plenty of stools, is absolutely the heart of this home. And there is an easy flow between the cooking space and the adjacent living area with a custom dining table and large fireplace. In the master bathroom shower, American-made Moroccan tile from Pratt & Larson adds a subtle but playful shot of pattern and texture, juxtaposed against the vintage brass wall-mounted soap shelf.

The topography of the narrow canyon, and the plentiful trees, mean that sunlight is a precious commodity, and homes in the neighborhood may feel dark and a little chilly. In order to capitalize on all available light, clerestory windows and skylights were necessary. The oculus, a circular skylight over the second-story landing, gives the stairwell a more open, airy feeling and is a natural spotlight for a Curtis Jeré hanging brass sculpture, and it casts the most incredible shadows on the floor and the walls as the sun passes through.

10 | MIRACLE MILE

It's always a thrill when clients task us with the challenge of designing a "dream house" that we build together from the ground up, selecting every finish and material. We had the pleasure of working on this contemporary home with clean, modern lines, and the focus was building the residential equivalent of an old soul, creating a meaningful balance between new materials, history, and character.

Located in the heart of Los Angeles in the Miracle Mile district, which was designed in the 1930s to be the city's premiere retail destination, the area is dotted with Art Deco landmarks and local cultural institutions. Close to LACMA, the La Brea Tar Pits, and the Original Farmers Market, the district features streets filled with modest bungalows from that era and newer, more modern homes on compact, tidy lots. This three-bedroom house maximizes every square foot, thanks to plenty of custom cabinetry and millwork in white oak. Other details include tongue and groove walls and interesting stone finishes—travertine, limestone, and marble—in the bathrooms and kitchen.

We adore designing kitchens. It's an exciting challenge to build a space that truly reflects how people live and function in their home. Open marble shelving and bronze cast hardware, made-to-order in Idaho by Sun Valley Bronze, are as distinct as they are functional. In the living room, the mismatched sculptural chairs in front of the fireplace look like they are having a conversation, or are distant members of the same family. Color makes a cameo appearance in the form of ochre mohair upholstery, woven black and tan Indian bed linens, and abstract paintings in shades of brick and burgundy.

Necessity breeds invention, even in interior design. When faced with the inconvenience of a too-close neighboring house, we designed a stained-glass window, inspired by glasswork we spotted on a trip to Milan and the angular grace of Frank Lloyd Wright or Mondrian, to hide it. The pattern on the window panel provides privacy without heavy-looking drapery and doesn't obscure the light. Its presence also carves an intriguing nook out of a hallway that may have otherwise been ignored.

BIOGRAPHY

Headed by principals Krista Schrock and David John Dick, DISC Interiors is an interior and furniture design firm based in Los Angeles. DISC Interiors strives to create homes of calibrated simplicity that balance the push and pull of modern life, address a sense of place and persons rather than any particular period or style, and balance the traditional with the modern and aesthetics with function. The homes they design are filled with vintage furniture and rugs juxtaposed against custom upholstery to feel contemporary yet classic and familiar. The projects designed by DISC Interiors represent a one-of-a-kind combination of traditional details and contemporary elegance.

ACKNOWLEDGMENTS

We are ever so grateful to our team, a small family that we delight in working with everyday. Their kindness, support, and love of the craft of design bring life to our projects. To Andisheh Shabani, Emilee Malvehy, Marissa Provenzano, Adria Pauli, Kelly Gomez, Taylor Dent, Tala Oliver Mateo, and Amy Wolfe, thank you.

Thanks also to Rizzoli's publisher, Charles Miers, and our editor, Ron Broadhurst, for allowing us to share our story, believing in our work, and trusting our vision.

To Mary Shanahan for your guidance, wisdom, and warmth, and Christine Lennon for your words and beautiful ways to tell a story.

To Sam Frost for your visual poetry and laughter, and to David Gilbert and Laure Joliet for your artistry included in this book.

To Glenn Lawson and Grant Fenning for your friendship and early encouragement.

To the architects, builders, artisans, furniture makers, and all those creating with their hands and minds—to collaborate everyday with you is pure joy.

To our clients over the years who trusted, encouraged, and allowed us to create a home for you.

And lastly to RJ Kaufman and Paul Bennett for your continual support, endless love, and encouragement.

First published in the United States of America in 2021 by
Rizzoli International Publications, Inc.
300 Park Avenue South
New York, NY 10010
www.rizzoliusa.com

© 2021 David John Dick and Krista Schrock

Book Design: Mary Shanahan

Publisher: Charles Miers
Editor: Ron Broadhurst
Production Manager: Barbara Sadick
Managing Editor: Lynn Scrabis

Printed and bound in China

2021 2022 2023 2024 2025 / 10 9 8 7 6 5 4 3 2 1

ISBN: 978-0-8478-6998-5
Library of Congress Control Number: 2020947761

Visit us online:
Facebook.com/RizzoliNewYork
Twitter: @Rizzoli_Books
Instagram.com/RizzoliBooks
Pinterest.com/RizzoliBooks
Youtube.com/user/RizzoliNY
Issuu.com/Rizzoli